Journey Along a River

The Amazon

Jen Green

WAYLAND

This book is a differentiated text version of A River Journey The Amazon by Simon Scoones.

This edition first published in 2009 by Wayland
Copyright © 2009 Wayland

Reprinted in 2010 by Wayland

This paperback edition published in 2012 by Wayland

Wayland
338 Euston Road
London NW1 3BH

Wayland
Level 17/207 Kent Street
Sydney NSW 2000

Editor: Victoria Brooker
Designer: Stephen Prosser

Brtish Cataloguing in Publication Data
Green, Jen.
  The Amazon. -- (Journey along a river)
  1. Amazon River--Juvenile literature. 2. Amazon River
  Valley--Juvenile literature.
  I. Title II. Series
  918.1'1-dc22

ISBN: 978 0 7502 8610 3

Printed in China

Wayland is a division of Hachette Children's Books,
an Hachette UK company.
www.hachette.co.uk

The website addresses (URLs) included in this book were valid at the time of going to press. However, because of the nature of the Internet, it is possible that some addresses may have changed, or sites may have changed or closed down since publication. While the author and Publisher regret any inconvenience this may cause readers, no responsibility for any such changes can be accepted by either the author or the Publisher.

Picture Acknowledgements

Cover and page 12: Tony Morrison/South American Pictures; title page Michel Roggo/Still Pictures; 2 Edward Parker/Still Pictures; 5 Jane Hawkins; 6 Simon Scoones; 7 Simon Scoones; 8 top Simon Scoones, below Panos/A. Bungeroth; 9 South American Pictures/Tony Morrison, inset Art Wolfe/Science Photo Library; 10 Simon Scoones, inset Richard Packwood/Oxford Scientific Films; 11 Tony Morrison/South American Pictures; 13 left Tony Morrison/South American Pictures, right South American Pictures; 14 Tony Morrison/South American Pictures, Simon Scoones; 15 Hart/Reflejo; 16 Dr Morley Read/Science Photo Library; 17 left Sinclair Stammers/Science Photo Library, right Partridge Films Ltd/Oxford Scientific Films; 18 Fred Hoogervorst/Panos; 19 Arabella Cecil/Panos; 20 Julia Waterlow/Eye Ubquitous; 21 left Edward Parker/Still Pictures, right Sue Cunningham/ SCP; 22 Simon Scoones; 23 top Edward Parker/Still Pictures, bottom Gregory Ochocki/Science Photo Library; 24 top Douglas Faulkner/Science Photo Library, bottom Kevin Schafer/Still Pictures; 25 Steve Bowles/ South American Pictures, bottom K. Gillham/Robert Harding; 26 Tony Morrison/South American Pictures; 27 top Edward Parker/Still Pictures, right Simon Scoones; 28 Robert Harding; 29 Mark Edwards/Still Pictures, inset Edward Parker/ South American Pictures; 30 Ken Gillham/Robert Harding; 31 Jean Chrisstophe Vie/Still Pictures; 32 K. Gillham/ Robert Harding, inset Simon Scoones; 33 Sue Cunningham/SCP, bottom Karen Ward/South American Pictures; 34 Ken Gillham/Robert Harding; 35 Tony Morrison/South American Pictures; 36 Jevan Berrange, inset Hellier Mason/Still Pictures; 38 Nigel Dickinson/Still Pictures; 39 top Geospace/Science Photo Library, inset Herbert Giradet/Still Pictures, bottom Topham Picture Point; 40 Martin Wendler/Still Pictures; 41 Sue Cunningham/ SCP; 42 left Jacques Jangoux/Science Photo Library, right Tony Allen/Oxford Scientific Films; 43 Tony Morrison/ South American Pictures; 44 Ken Gillham/Robert Harding; 45 left Mark Edwards/Still Pictures, right NASA/Still Pictures

Contents

Words in **bold** can be found in the glossary on page 47.

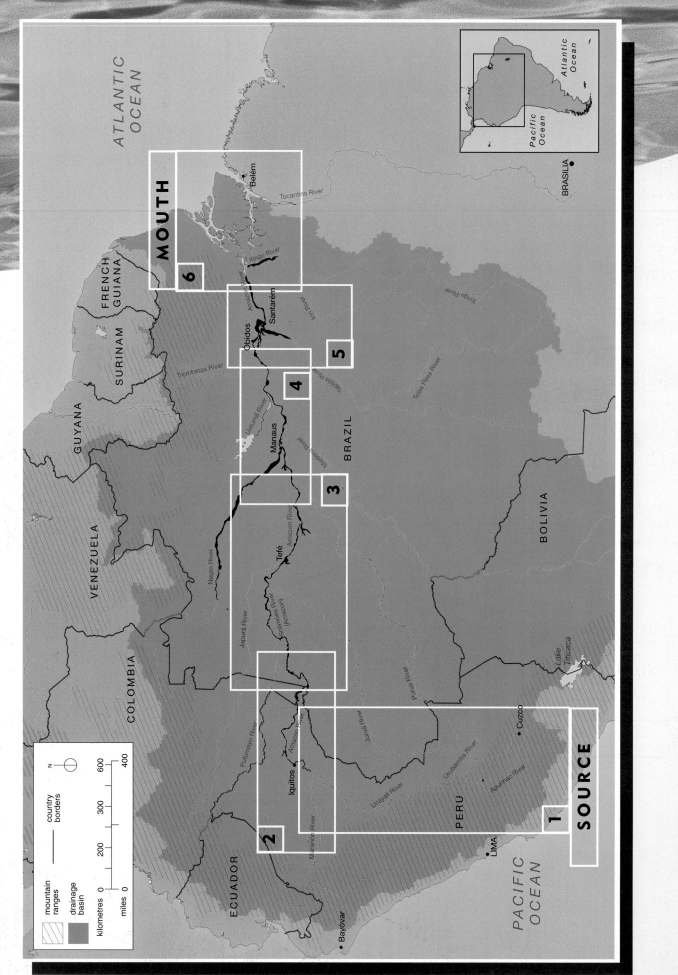

Your guide to the river

Using the maps

The River Amazon is one of the world's longest rivers. It contains more water than any other river. About a quarter of all the fresh water in the world flows along this mighty river. The Amazon drains a vast area, covering one third of South America. The map on page 4 shows the whole length of the Amazon River. The white squares show how our journey along the river has been divided into six chapters.

Map references

Each chapter has a map showing the part of the river we have reached. The numbered boxes show where places of interest are found.

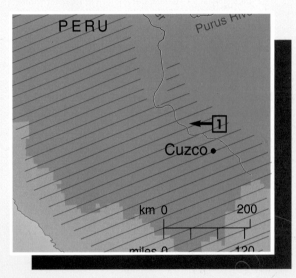

The journey ahead

We are following the River Amazon from its beginnings to the sea. The distance is over 5,000 kilometres! Our journey begins high in the Andes Mountains in Peru. Here the Urubamba River, which feeds the Amazon, is born. We follow the river north as it gushes down steep slopes, and then winds through a huge rainforest. Beyond the city of Iquitos the Amazon heads east, and finally reaches the Atlantic Ocean. Where it meets the ocean the river is so wide you cannot see the far bank.

Our journey begins on foot in the snowy peaks of the Andes. Wear hiking boots, and wrap up warm!

Nauta •

Marañon River

Juruá River

BRAZIL

Ucayali River

Urubamba River

Purus River

PERU

1

Cuzco •

km 0   200

miles 0   120

1. A river with many beginnings

It is hard to say exactly where the Amazon begins because it is fed by so many rivers. The streams and rivers that join it are called tributaries. It probably begins on the high plains of the Andes. Here melted snow and rain drain off the peaks to form the Urubamba River.

▼ **The ancient city of Machu Picchu perches high on a ridge above the Urubamba River.**

▲ The Incas were very skilful builders. Their beautifully carved stone walls still stand.

▶ The rushing waters of the Urubamba carve a deep valley as they tumble downhill.

Valley of the Incas

As we head **downstream** we pass through the Urubamba River valley. It is known as the sacred valley of the Incas, because it was settled by a people called the Incas about 800 years ago.

The Incas developed farming techniques to cope with the steep **terrain**. They cut little steps into hillsides to make flat areas called terraces. They watered these fields by sending river water through channels carved in the rock.

The Incas developed an advanced civilisation. They built fine cities throughout their empire. The cities were linked by stone paths running through the mountains. Inca traders used the paths to bring food and other goods to the cities. However, the Incas were conquered by the Spanish in the 1500s, and their civilisation was destroyed.

Machu Picchu

We visit the amazing ancient city of Machu Picchu MAP REF 1. After the Spanish conquest the city remained hidden for 500 years. In 1911 an American **archaeologist** called Hiram Bingham rediscovered it after a tip-off from a local farmer. Now thousands of tourists visit every year.

▲ The Incas used to try out new crops on these terraces. The person in the middle shows how big this area is.

◀ A Quechua girl with an alpaca. Her hat and shawl are made from alpaca wool.

Potatoes and pack animals

In the Urubamba valley we meet the local people, called the Quechua. Quechua is also the name of an Inca language. Many Quechua people are descended from the Incas.

The Quechua farm the valley as the Incas did before them. They grow different crops together and also vary crops from year to year. This method of farming does not harm the soil.

The Quechua grow more than 400 types of potato! They also rear herds of woolly llama and alpaca. Llamas can carry heavy loads and are also reared for meat. The llama's woolly cousin, the alpaca, is another useful animal. Alpacas produce fine wool, which the Quechua weave into warm clothing.

A hard life

The **climate** of this region is harsh, especially in winter. Some Quechuas have left the hard life of farming. They have moved to towns lower down the valley where they sell goods to tourists.

Cloud forest

We **descend** through a forest high above the river. This region receives up to six metres of rain a year. This mountainous forest is called cloud forest because it is always swathed in clouds and mist.

The cloud forest acts like a giant sponge, holding moisture. Water drips off trees and plants. Moisture rising into the air forms clouds, which shed more rain. In this way, water circles constantly between the air and land.

▲ **Ferns and colourful orchids sprout high on trees. This is a cock-of-the-rock bird.**

A magical world

Walking through the cloud forest is like entering a magical garden. Plants sprout from every branch and treetrunk. There are more types of plant here than in the whole of Europe. The cloud forest has special animals, too. Frogs croak from streams and pools. We may be lucky enough to spot a scarlet cock-of-the-rock bird, performing a mating dance.

Raging water

The Urubamba twists through a narrow **gorge** as it heads north. It leaves the mountains and enters the foothills. Here its name changes and it becomes the Ucayali River. The loss of height gives the river energy. The gushing water carries loose rocks, soil and branches along with it. These help to wear away the bed, deepening the gorge. Foaming rapids form where the torrent crashes into rocks. The rocks form perches for birds as they search for fish in the waters below.

Warm, sticky weather

As we descend the air becomes warmer. The Sun's heat causes moisture to rise into the air to form thunderclouds. Heavy downpours are common. As we reach the hot, sticky lowlands, the cloud forest gives way to tropical rainforest.

► **A kingfisher perches above the river, searching for fish.**

▼ **Rapids form where the river smashes into boulders on its bed.**

Indians of the Amazon

American Indians (known as Amerindians) have lived in the rainforest for thousands of years. When Europeans first explored the Amazon **basin** in the 1500s, about two million Amerindians were living in the forest.

Today, only about 250,000 Amerindians are left. Some were killed by Europeans as they took over much of this region. Others were forced to become slaves, and died of overwork. Many died of diseases such as measles, brought by Europeans.

Varied cultures

During our journey we will meet many Amerindian groups. Each has its own traditions and way of life. Some groups live in villages, while others wander the forest. At least fifty groups have had no contact with outsiders. They still live a traditional way of life, as their people have lived for hundreds of years.

A new name

Near the town of Nauta in eastern Peru is a landmark on our journey.

▲ **This Amerindian is a member of a group from Peru.**

Here the Ucayali River meets the Marañón River, which also began high in the Andes. The Marañón has journeyed 1, 800 kilometres to reach this point. The two join to make a river which is called the Amazon for the first time.

Amerindians build log rafts. We take one of these as we head north through the rainforest. Don't forget your paddle!

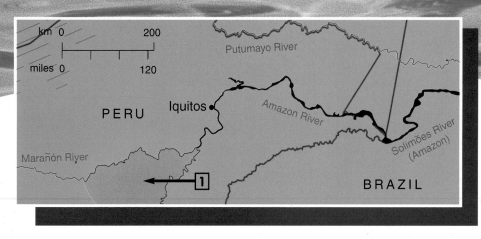

2. The Upper Amazon

Many smaller rivers join the Amazon in the lowlands of Peru. Most have already made long journeys from areas to the north or west. The land is now very flat, but the flow is still powerful, because the river is fed by water pouring off the mountains. The channel is deep and wide at the city of Iquitos.

▼ **As the river curves it wears away the outside of bends and drops silt on the inside. Bends develop into deep loops.**

▲ The Yagua people live near Iquitos. Christian missionaries tried to convert them, but they held onto their own religion and language.

▲ Spanish missionaries tried to make the Amerindians become Christians. This old illustration shows a Spanish priest preaching to Indians.

Exploring the river

The river weaves from side to side like a snake. It has worn away the land to form deep loops called **meanders**. These loops add to our journey as we paddle along the river, so we only make slow progress.

A Spanish soldier named Francisco de Orellana was the first European to reach this part of the Amazon, in 1541. He was surprised to find large Indian villages by the river. Like many Europeans of his time, he thought Amerindians were uncivilised. In fact, they were very intelligent. They had a well-developed culture and thorough understanding of the natural world.

Missionaries

Later, European missionaries came to try to **convert** the Amerindians to Christianity. But the Indians had their own beliefs. Their gods were linked to nature. They did not accept Christianity and even killed some missionaries with poison darts.

No roads to Iquitos

We drift downriver to reach Iquitos. This city has around 400,000 people. It is the largest city in the world that cannot be reached by road. The only way to get there is by boat or plane. There are very few cars in Iquitos, but bicycles, motorbikes and three-seater motor carts fill the streets. Ferries carry goods and people across the river. The river is already deep and wide, so boats can travel all the way to the Atlantic Ocean, 3,700 kilometres away.

Busy markets

The centre of Iquitos is busy. Markets by the river sell fruit, vegetables, fish, tobacco and timber. People come from villages around to sell their produce. At food stalls you can try palmeta, a fish soup. Local delicacies include turtle-meat soup and fried monkey!

◀ **Pedal power is important in Iquitos because there are very few cars.**

▼ **These fruit are cashew apples. The flesh can be squeezed to make delicious juice.**

▲ **Thatched huts by the river in Iquitos. The river level is low here – imagine what happens in the rainy season!**

Coping with floods

The water level in the Amazon rises in the wet season. The people of Iquitos have to cope with changing water levels. Thousands of people live on low-lying land by the river. Their makeshift homes are made of timber and corrugated iron.

When the river rises people use canoes instead of bicycles to get about. People build their homes on stilts to avoid getting flooded. Other homes are made of light balsa wood and can float.

Drilling for oil

Rich stocks of oil and gas lie underground in this part of the Amazon. Iquitos is the centre of the oil industry in the Amazon basin. Oil has become big business. The United States buys a lot of oil from the region.

Crude oil pumped from the ground goes by pipeline or barge to a refinery near Iquitos. There the crude oil is heated and refined to produce gasoline and kerosene. The refined oil is pumped right over the Andes. A very long pipeline takes it west to the port of Bayóvar on the Pacific coast, 800 kilometres away.

Problems with oil

Oil has brought money and jobs to the Amazon. But it also brings the risk of pollution. In October 2000, 5,500 barrels of oil spilled into the Marañón River. A vast area was polluted. The oil spill damaged the nearby Pacaya Samiria Reserve MAP REF 1, Peru's largest protected area. Plants and wildlife died. Around 20,000 people depend on the river for food. The spilled oil poisoned or suffocated large numbers of fish, so fish catches became much smaller. Local people went hungry. Many Indians also developed health problems after drinking or washing in polluted water.

The Urarina people

The Urarina are a shy and peaceful group of Amerindians. They settled around the Marañón River centuries ago. They live by clearing small gardens in the swampy forest where they grow corn, manioc and banana. They catch fish and hunt forest animals using blowpipes. Now the Urarina way of life is threatened by contact with outsiders.

◀ **An oil drilling area in the Amazon. The dark square is an abandoned oil well.**

▼ **An oil pipeline runs through part of the forest that has recently been cleared.**

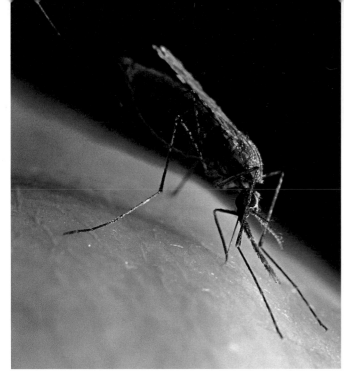

▲ Mosquitoes can carry malaria. People who are bitten by the mosquito can catch malaria.

▶ A saki monkey. Poachers hunt these monkeys for their bushy tails, which are sold as dusters.

Outside contact

Oil companies enter the region to search for oil. Tourists have also arrived. The Urarina are not used to contact with outsiders. They have no natural protection from dangerous diseases such as influenza. In recent years many Urarina have died from diseases caught from outsiders, and also from malaria and **cholera**.

Poachers

Poachers are another problem. They enter Urarina land to hunt the local saki monkeys. But the Urarina have formed their own bands of guards, called 'river wolves'. These men patrol the forest to keep poachers at bay. They also try to stop poachers putting poison in the river to catch fish. The poison kills all wildlife in that part of the river.

We now ride in a dug-out canoe towards the three-way border between Peru, Colombia and Brazil. There we will enter Brazil.

Japurá River

Negro River

Putumayo River

Solimões River
(Amazon)

1

Tefé

Amazon River

Juruá River

km 0   200

miles 0   120

BRAZIL

Purus River

3. The Amazon Rainforest

As we enter Brazil, the river's name changes again. Along this stretch it is called the Solimões. All around us is a vast rainforest which is rich in plant and animal life.

◀ **The forest is home to a huge range of plants.**

▼ **Buttress roots stick out to support the weight of the tree.**

A lush world

The river snakes east for hundreds of kilometres, through a dense forest. The Amazon Rainforest is very special. A tenth of the world's plant and animal species live here. The Amazon Rainforest lies close to the Equator. Trees and plants can grow all year round in the hot, wet conditions here. The forest trees spread their roots underground to suck up water and **nutrients**. They use the nutrients to grow to amazing heights. The very tallest trees, such as kapok trees, grow to 40 metres tall.

A thick layer of leaves shades the ground and protects it from downpours. The trees act like an umbrella which protects the forest plants and animals. Plants and vines grow along the branches of giant trees. The trees also provide **habitats** for animals and birds.

▲ **A scarlet macaw flies over a patch of water lilies. The enormous leaves can measure over two metres across.**

Cycle of life

Down on the forest floor, dead plants and animals rot quickly. Insects and fungi help to break down their remains. The nutrients they contain return to the soil for trees and plants to use again.

River life

Rainwater drains into the river from the forest. It carries nutrients into the river to nourish the creatures there. Scientists believe up to 3,000 types of fish live in the river. The murky depths are home to strange transparent catfish, and blind fish that hunt using electricity. Water lilies spread across the surface in calm stretches. Nimble birds use the lily pads as stepping stones as they search for insects.

Living in the forest

The Amerindians along this stretch of river have a deep understanding of the forest. They know that the soil becomes **infertile** if they plant crops in one place year after year. So they move to another patch of forest to give the soil a chance to recover.

Most Amerindians use canoes to get about, whether visiting friends or going to work or school. Canoes are carved from a single tree trunk. When not in use, people fill them with water. This helps to prevent the wood from drying out and splitting.

In times of war, some Indian groups used to carve large canoes from mighty forest trees. These could hold up to 30 warriors. Canoes are also used to hunt pirarucu, the world's largest freshwater fish.

Using the forest

Amerindians mostly use forest **resources** without cutting down trees. One tree's bark makes very strong rope. The **sap** from another makes a firelighter. Vivid dyes are made from seeds, bark and leaves. These dyes are used to decorate the body. Soft spongy leaves are even used as toilet paper!

▲ These men have caught a small pirarucu. These fish grow up to four metres long.

◄ A boy paddles by in his canoe.

► This child's skin is painted with vegetable dyes. The red dye on his face is made from seeds.

Amerindian groups also use the forest to make music. They carve flutes from bamboo or animal leg bones. Hollow gourds, made from dried pumpkin skins, are filled with seeds to make musical instruments called maracas. The sound of pairs of maracas is heard at festivals all over Brazil.

Reserves

To protect the lands of the Amerindians, the governments of the Amazon basin have created reserves. There are now about 30 reserves in the Amazon basin. These help to **preserve** the forest groups and their way of life. Traditions and customs pass from parents to children.

Rising waters

Rain falls all year round in the Amazon basin. There is also an extra-rainy season between January and March. We pass through areas called igapos, which are flooded all year round.

During the wet season new parts of the forest flood. The swollen river rises 20 metres and floods an area the size of England. At this time the Amazon holds more water than the world's eight next biggest rivers combined. As water spills over the land, fish and other water creatures explore new parts of the forest.

▲ **In the wet season, you need a boat to explore the flooded forest.**

The flooded forest

Caimans, cousins of alligators, hunt their prey among the reeds. Fruit-eating fish help to spread plant seeds. They eat fleshy fruits that drop into the water. The seeds pass right through their bodies and are dropped to sprout elsewhere.

High in the **canopy**, monkeys leap from tree to tree, feeding on leaves and fruit. The white uacari monkey can leap 30 metres. It has no fur on its head, and its face is bright red. Sloths move much more slowly than monkeys, but are surprisingly good swimmers.

October brings drier weather. The river level drops and much of the flooded forest becomes dry again. Some **channels** of water are cut off to become small lakes.

▼ **Uacari monkeys feed on unripe fruit in the flooded forest.**

A handsome dolphin

The pink dolphin or bôto lives in the flooded forest. It feeds off fish in the igapos. This is the only dolphin that can bend its neck. Local people have a legend about the dolphin.

In June people gather to celebrate the feast of St John by eating and dancing. The bôto is said to visit the party disguised as a handsome young man. He wears a hat to hide the nostrils on top of his head.

The bôto dances with a beautiful woman. He tries to persuade her to join him at the bottom of the river. Any man who is wearing a hat will be asked to remove it, to check he is not a bôto!

▼ **The bôto is almost blind. It hunts fish by sending out clicking sounds and listening for echoes.**

▲ **Manatees are gentle and curious. They grow up to three metres long.**

◀ **Scarlet macaws sometimes eat clay from the river bank. Minerals in the clay probably help them digest poisons in their food.**

During the wet season, the river rises 12 metres. This becomes the largest flooded forest reserve in Brazil.

The Mamiraua

The Japurá River joins the Solimões River, on which we are travelling, near the town of Tefé. A wildlife reserve called the Mamiraua MAP REF 1 lies in the watery triangle between the two rivers.

People and the Mamiraua

Mamiraua is the local word for a baby manatee. Manatees are large, rare mammals that live in the river. They have seal-like bodies and powerful flat tails. The Mamiraua Reserve helps to protect rare species. It also helps to preserve the way of life of local people. About 5,000 local people live in parts of the reserve, which is unusual. Most reserves contain few people, and plants and animals are strictly protected. However, here local people are allowed to fish and collect wood. They also help to manage the reserve.

Medicines and poisons

About eighty scientists study local plants and animals. Scientists have discovered that some rainforest plants can be used as medicines. Amerindian groups have used these medicines for centuries. The bark of one tree contains quinine, which helps to cure **malaria**.

Some plant foods are nourishing. A fruit called guaraná gives you extra energy. Nowadays it is ground up and made into milkshakes. The cacao tree produces fruit pods that are used to make chocolate.

Not all plants are healing or nourishing. A plant called curare yields poison. Amerindians tip their blowpipe darts in

▲ **A scientist collects plant samples in the Mamiraua Reserve.**

the poison before they go on a monkey hunt. If a monkey high in a tree is struck by a poisoned dart, it soon drops to the ground.

Our next stop, Manaus, is a long way away. We ride on one of the paddle steamers that have travelled the river for years.

4. The meeting of the waters

Manaus is the biggest city in the Amazon basin. Near here the Solimões River meets the Rio Negro – the Black River. The Solimões is white from silt washed from the mountains. The Negro is black from rotting leaves. The waters flow side by side and then mix. From now on the river is called the Amazon.

▼ **The white waters of the Solimões meet the black waters of the Rio Negro.**

Villages of the plain

The flat land on either side of the river is called the várzea or floodplain. Local people grow crops here and live in houses on stilts. In the wet season, the river spreads over the floodplain, dropping fertile **silt**. People move upstairs in their stilt houses. Fish is an important food for every várzea family. Children learn to fish almost before they can walk.

▲ Preparing manioc is a long, complicated process. Everyone in the village helps.

▶ Palm berries in a basket woven from palm leaves. The berries are crushed to make wine.

Farming the floodplain

When the floods go down, people plant crops in the fertile soil. The most important crop is a root called manioc. When the manioc **tubers** (roots) are big enough, farmers dig them up, peel them and boil them to make a pulp. They squeeze out the liquid to get rid of poisons. The pulp is dried, then pounded into a flour called farinha. The flour is used to make bread.

Forest skills

Many people of the várzea are of mixed race. Their ancestors were Amerindian, European and African. They are called Caboclos. The Caboclos use the skills of their Amerindian ancestors. They build temporary shelters in the forest with thatched roofs made of palm leaves. These shelters stay dry even in heavy rain. They sleep in hammocks slung from hooks fixed to the shelter's wooden beams.

The rubber boom

About 150 years ago, people in Manaus struck it rich. They discovered that sticky **latex** sap from rubber trees could be made into rubber. The invention of tyres in Europe made rubber as valuable as gold.

Steamboats carried the rubber downstream to the Atlantic coast. From there ships carried it to Europe. Manaus became a major port. It expanded very rapidly between 1865 and 1900.

▼ **The coloured dome of the opera house in Manaus still stands out. But now it is surrounded by skyscrapers.**

Great wealth

Rubber brought great riches to Manaus. Wealthy rubber traders built fine mansions. The opera house, built in 1856, was another symbol of the new wealth. It is made of wrought iron and Italian stone. It is decorated with 36,000 beautiful French tiles and lit by crystal chandeliers.

However, by the early 1900s British traders had smuggled rubber seeds out of South America. They set up rival rubber plantations in South-east Asia. Brazil's rubber boom was over.

▲ **These rubber tappers are members of a union which protects their way of life.**

▶ **A rubber tapper slices the bark of a rubber tree. The milky sap will drip into a cup fixed to the tree.**

Tapping rubber

The rubber boom may be over, but many people still work as rubber tappers. Each tapper looks after about 200 rubber trees. Every day the tapper takes a trail through the forest. He or she sets little cups to catch the latex. The tapper takes a different trail home, collecting latex from a previous trip.

Back at home the tapper heats the latex. It is mixed with vinegar to make it solid. The latex mix is sold to a rubber trader.

Chico Mendes

Chico Mendes is the hero of the rubber tappers. Chico saw that cattle ranchers were taking over, and cutting down, the forests containing rubber trees. Chico came up with the idea of setting up rubber reserves. These are areas set aside for collecting rubber and other forest products without cutting down trees. A fierce struggle developed between the ranchers and the rubber tappers. In 1988 Chico was killed by his enemies. But his reserves still protect the forest and the rubber tappers.

New industries

Nowadays rubber is less important, but Manaus is still doing well. The city has become a 'free trade zone'. This means foreign businesses do not pay taxes on goods coming in and out of Manaus, which saves them money.

Manaus has become an important centre for electronics. Over 400 electronics factories have set up here. These, and other businesses, can either use the river to transport their goods, or the goods can go by plane. An airport has been built nearby. However, there are also problems. As factories update their equipment, fewer workers are needed. So, some people have lost their jobs.

▲ **The docks at Manaus are built to cope with dramatic changes in the river level.**

River power

Local industries, such as electronics, create a demand for energy. The Amazon is too wide and slow to be used to **generate** energy. But about eighty tributaries feed into it. These fast-flowing rivers can be dammed to produce **hydroelectric** power.

To produce the electricity a dam is built. A large lake called a **reservoir** forms as water builds up behind the dam. The dam increases the flow of water past giant wheels called **turbines**. These spin to work machines called generators, which produce electricity.

A harmful dam

This technology is not always successful. In 1987 the Balbina Dam MAP REF 1 was completed on the Uatumã River near Manaus. Water built up behind the dam. But because the land was fairly flat it flooded a huge area.

Many people think the Balbina Dam is a disaster. Amerindians who lived there were forced to leave to make way for the reservoir. But they weren't even offered new land or money in exchange.

The new lake has become a swamp. Mosquitoes carrying diseases such as malaria breed there. Dead vegetation rots in the water, releasing gases that cause pollution. The flat landscape means that the water does not flow fast enough to produce much electricity. The Balbina Dam only produces a third of the energy that the experts planned.

▼ **Dead trees rot in the lake behind the Balbina Dam. The lake is so shallow land breaks the surface here and there.**

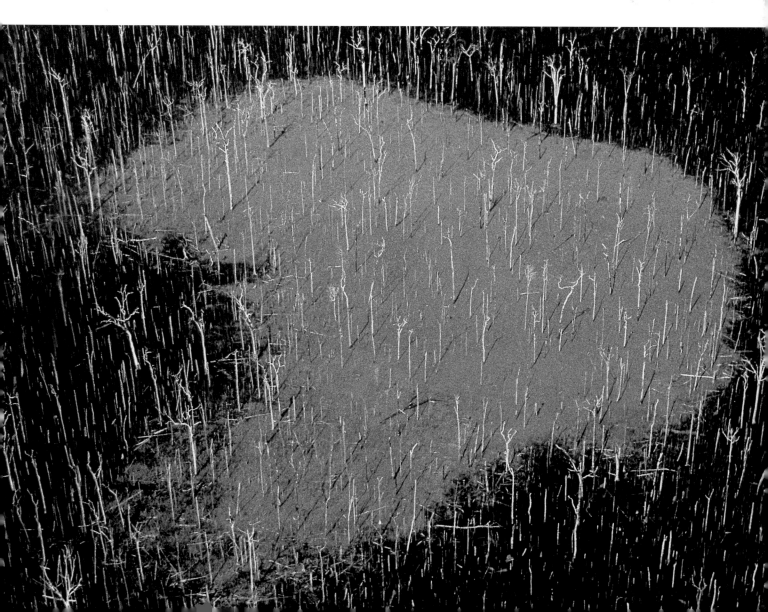

Ecotourism

Manaus is a growing centre for **ecotourism**. This type of tourism aims to bring in money without harming the **environment**. Traditional ways of life are preserved. New jobs are also created, running hotels, restaurants and boats.

We leave the ferry and take a trip to an ecolodge on Silves Island MAP REF 2. Some of the money from lodges like this is used to protect nature, and also help local people. However some ecolodges are owned by foreign companies, so most of the money goes abroad.

We take a van to the end of the road. The lodge is then a five-hour journey upriver by voadeira – motorised canoe. We hear the call of the japin as we cruise upriver. This bird copies the songs of other birds. We try to catch piranha fish using meat as bait.

The forest at night

We reach the lodge at dusk. You need to be brave to enter the flooded forest at night! There are tarantula spiders, snakes and caimans. Their eyes glint red when you shine your torch into the dark.

◄ **This piranha will make a tasty meal for a tourist. Amerinidans don't eat piranhas. But they do use their sharp teeth to file their nails.**

▼ **Western tourists at an ecolodge in the forest. This lookout tower helps visitors to spot birds.**

Welcome to Ariaú Jungle Tower

Bem vindo ao Ariaú

A dance contest

Tourists also come to sample the rich culture of the region. A festival called the Boi Bumbá, or Ox Dance, is held on Parintins Island MAP REF 3 each year in June.

The festival tells the story of Catirina and her husband, Francisco. Catirina had a craving for ox-tongue. Francisco killed his master's ox to keep her happy. But he was thrown in prison for his crime. Later he was saved when a magician called Pajé brought the ox back to life.

Each year two dance groups from Manaus perform the story. After three days of singing and dancing, the judges choose the winner. The winning group and their supporters celebrate.

▼ **Dancers perform the Ox Dance on Parintins Island.**

We still have a long journey to the Atlantic coast. We buy hammocks so we can sleep on the ferry.

5. The Amazon floodplain

Beyond Manaus we continue east along the Amazon. The river is muddy-brown because of all the silt in it. Near the town of Santarém, a **tributary** called the Tapajós River joins us. Its water is clear blue because it contains little silt.

▼ **This sandbank is made from silt dropped by the river.**

The Óbidos Narrows

Earth's outer crust is made up of huge rigid plates that drift very slowly across the surface. Millions of years ago, movement of these plates created a deep channel between two mountain ranges. It was filled with water flowing toward the Atlantic.

Today this channel is the Óbidos Narrows MAP REF 1. The river shrinks to a third of its width as it passes through the narrows. This makes the water flow faster. This is the deepest, narrowest point on the river in Brazil. The Narrows form a natural gateway on the last stage of our journey to the ocean.

Guarding the Narrows

The Portuguese ruled Brazil in the 1600s. They built a fort at Óbidos. Here the river is so narrow you can see the far bank, so the Portuguese could watch for

▲ **The clear blue waters of the Tapajós River join the Amazon near the town of Santarém.**

enemies. Óbidos was once the largest town on this stretch of river. It is less important now, but the old fort is a tourist attraction.

Silt and tides

The vast **floodplain** on either side of us is very flat. The river has dropped huge amounts of silt. The silt forms sandy beaches on inside bends of the river, where the **current** is slow. Much of this land floods in the wet season.

We are still 800 kilometres from the coast. But high ocean tides can push water this far up the river. Over the years, sea creatures such as stingrays have drifted upstream with the tides. They now thrive here, having adjusted to a new freshwater habitat.

Buried treasure

The land around the river here is rich in minerals. This treasure includes copper, **bauxite** and manganese. There is also gold. More than a million people have come to the Amazon in search of gold. Huge tracts of forest have been felled by the miners. With the abundant rainfall, these areas become mud baths in which people dig for gold. The life of a gold-miner is hard, and most people leave empty-handed.

▶ **A local worker shows how the silt from the river bed may hold precious minerals, such as gold.**

36

Gold mining

The Tapajós Valley is the largest gold-mining area in the Amazon basin. Specks of gold are found in the river silt. Gold-diggers add liquid mercury to separate the gold from silt.

Unfortunately, mercury is poisonous. Some mercury rises into the air, causing pollution. Most drains into the river, where it is absorbed by fish. People who eat the fish can get mercury poisoning. You can also be poisoned by breathing polluted air. Mercury poisoning causes serious health problems such as brain damage. Thousands of people who live along the Tapajós River have mercury poisoning, caused by either eating fish or breathing mercury in the air.

Dredging the Tapajós

There are plans to **dredge** the final section of the Tapajós River. The dredged section will run for 1,000 kilometres **upstream** from Santarém. Dredging will make the channel wider and deeper. Bigger cargo ships will be able to travel the Tapajós and then down the Amazon to the coast.

Local farmers will benefit from the scheme. They will be able to transport grain to overseas markets, such as Europe. The grain is sold as cattle feed. But some people worry that the dredging will churn up silt and pollute the river. Waste from the cargo ships could increase pollution. The dredging will also increase the risk of flooding from water surging down the river.

◀ **More than a million gold-miners work in the goldfields of the Amazon basin.**

▲ Cattle ranching damages the land. In just ten years, forest land can become a desert.

Clearing the Amazon

Since the 1970s, the Brazilian government has been encouraging people from overcrowded cities in Brazil to move to the Amazon basin. New roads have opened up remote areas, and linked river towns to the outside world.

The Trans-Amazonian Highway runs for 5,000 kilometres across the region. A new road links Santarém with the south MAP REF 2 . Other roads are made by logging companies cutting down trees **illegally**. Hardwood trees such as mahogany are very valuable. The timber is shipped to rich countries such as the United States.

New roads bring settlers to the region. The settlers clear patches of forest to grow food. Huge tracts of forest are also cleared to make way for new cattle ranches and plantations.

The disappearing forest

Satellite images of the region, such as the one on page 39, show that the forest is disappearing quickly. Nearly 700,000 square kilometres of rainforest in Brazil has been destroyed since 1970. That is an area the size of France and Greece. The destruction is speeding up. Nearly 20 per cent of the rainforest has now been destroyed.

'Advance Brazil'

Up to a quarter of the remaining rainforest in Brazil could be lost over the next twenty years. More roads, **dams** and pipelines are planned as part of a project called 'Advance Brazil'. Under this scheme the government plans to open up more of the Amazon basin for farming, mining and logging.

▲ **This satellite image shows part of the rainforest. The light-coloured patches have been cleared of trees.**

▶ **The destruction caused when the forest is cleared.**

Advance Brazil will create new jobs and bring in wealth for the whole country. But it could cost as much as 40 billion US dollars. And its effect on the rainforest could be disastrous.

The last stage of our journey takes us through the Amazon delta to the coast. We need an experienced guide to take us through the maze of watery channels.

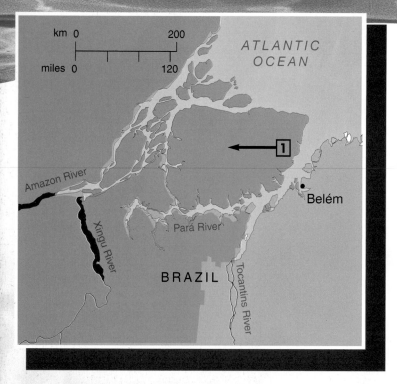

6. The Amazon delta

On the last stage of our journey the Amazon is deep and very wide. Every second, the river empties about 250 million litres of water into the Atlantic Ocean! As the current slows, the river drops its load of silt, to form a huge flat, swampy **delta**. We sail past islands in the delta to reach the port of Belém on the coast.

▼ **As the river nears the coast, it splits into many channels. These weave between islands made of silt.**

▲ These pots were made on Marajó Island.

▶ Drums feature in all kinds of Brazilian music. The Carimbó dance is named after a tall drum.

Skilful potters

Marajó Island MAP REF 1 is the largest island in the Amazon delta. It covers an area the size of Switzerland. People have lived on the island for 2,000 years.

Aruã Indians used to live on Marajó. These brave people fought the Portuguese when they claimed the region. But by the 1700s the Aruã had been wiped out.

The Aruã were skilful potters. Today, the people of Marajó Island still make pots in a similar way. They take clay from the river bank, shape it into pots, and bake it in the sun.

Songs of slaves

The music and dance of Marajó Island are influenced by a different culture. African slaves who ran away from the Portuguese hid on the island. Ex-slaves wrote the music for a dance called the Carimbó, which is still popular today. It is named after a drum.

Carimbó music is sad. The songs tell of the slaves' longing for their African homeland. But the dance is also fun. Men and women dance around in a big circle. When the women drop their handkerchiefs, the men have to pick them up with their teeth!

▲ **Capybaras dive underwater if danger threatens.**

◄ **The water around Marajó Island is brown with silt.**

Giant rodents

Marajó Island is only just above sea level. Parts of the island flood during the wet season. Capybaras look like giant guinea pigs. They can stand one metre tall and weigh up to sixty kilograms. They have webbed feet and are good swimmers. They spend a lot of time in the water. However, capybaras are becoming scarce because their habitat is shrinking. People also hunt them for food. Their flesh is said to be tasty.

Water buffalo

Farmers have cleared most of the trees in the east of the island to make new fields and grasslands. Rice, fruit, vegetables and also coconuts are grown. Cattle and water buffalo graze the pastures. According to local legend, water buffalo reached the island after a ship that was carrying them was wrecked. They do well on this marshy land because they don't mind swimming.

▲ Water buffalo are strong work animals. Their meat and hides are also sold.

▶ Coconut shells dry in the sun before the outer fibre is removed.

Cars and coconuts

Coconuts are plentiful on Marajó Island. Some local farmers have found a new way to make money from coconuts. They sell coconut fibre to a major car company. The hairy fibres from the coconut shells are used to fill the seats and head rests of cars sold in Brazil.

The farmers make good money from this new use of coconut. It is also good for the environment, because the fibres can be recycled. And they cause less pollution than the artificial fibres normally used if they are burned.

Surfing the wave

The ocean tides here at the mouth of the Amazon are very powerful around the full moon in February and March. The spring tides send a wave up to three metres high racing up the river. Surfers come to ride the wave. The ride can last up to 45 minutes!

A busy port

We reach the port of Belém, our final destination. The Portuguese founded Belém in 1616. Amerindian slaves, cocoa and spices from the Amazon basin sailed from here to the outside world.

Belém was also the base for Europeans bound for the Amazon. But there was fierce fighting between Europeans and Amerindians. Thousands of Amerindians were killed or forced into slavery. After centuries of hardship, slavery finally ended in Brazil in 1888.

During the 1900s, Belém grew wealthy from the rubber trade, like Manaus upriver. Today, all kinds of riches from the Amazon basin pass through the port. For example, timber from the rainforest passes through on its way abroad. Over 20 million cubic tonnes of timber are sold abroad each year. About two million people live in and around Belém.

Belém market

We visit the Ver-o-Peso market in Belém. The name means 'See the weight'. Slaves were once bought and sold at this market. Today all kinds of goods from the Amazon basin are on sale. The fish hall has fish for eating, and also tropical fish for aquariums. You can buy nuts, fruits and items such as sieves made from woven straw. You can even buy bottled snakes or charms to ward off evil spirits!

A tasty fruit

Down at the waterfront we watch açaí fruit being unloaded from large boats. Açaí is the fruit of a palm tree that grows on islands in the delta. Children climb the trees to harvest the bunches of fruit at the top. Açaí is mixed with manioc flour to make a delicious fruit 'smoothie'. Açaí ice cream is also tasty. Growing palm trees for açaí brings in money without cutting down trees.

▲ Açaí fruit are unloaded for sale at the market.

▶ This satellite photograph shows the mouth of the Amazon River. You can see brown river silt spreading out into the ocean.

▼ Timber is transported to market down the Amazon.

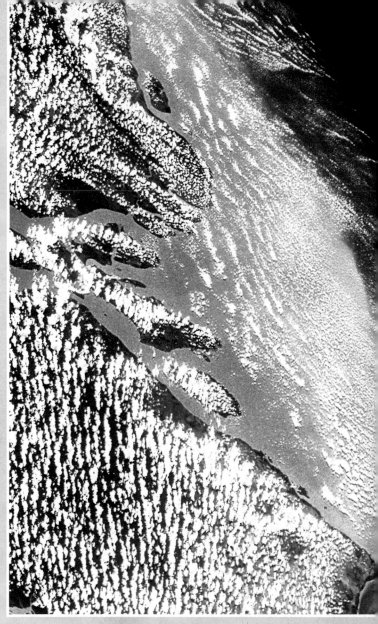

Journey's end

At the mouth of the Amazon, the river is 240 kilometres wide. The river is far too wide to see the opposite bank, so it looks like a sea. Every year the river carries over a million tonnes of silt into the Atlantic Ocean. Some of the silt has come from the high Andes Mountains where our journey began over 5,000 kilometres away.

A profile of the River Amazon, which falls very steeply on the first part of its journey to the Atlantic Ocean.

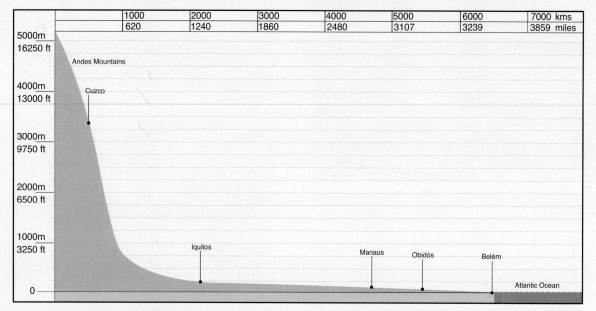

	1000	2000	3000	4000	5000	6000	7000 kms
	620	1240	1860	2480	3107	3239	3859 miles

Further information

Useful websites

http://www.amazonwatch.org/
Amazon Watch defends the environment and peoples of the Amazon basin.

http://www.korubo.com/
Tells the story of an exploration to find a remote Amazon people.

http://www.pbs.org/journeyintoamazonia/
A website that explores the wildlife of the Amazon basin.

http://www.pbs.org/wgbh/nova/shaman/
A website about the Yanomami people of the Amazon.

http://www.ran.org/
The website of the Rainforest Action Network – a campaign group which defends rainforests worldwide.

Books

Caring for the Planet: Tropical Rainforest by Neil Champion (Watts, 2006)

Eco Alert: Rainforests by Robert Hunter (Watts, 2010)

Food Chains in Action: Who Eats Who in the Rainforest? by Robert Endeen (Watts, 2009)

Global Questions: Why are Rainforests Being Destroyed? by Peter Littlewood (Watts, 2010)

Espresso Ideas Box: Rainforests by Deborah Chancellor (Watts, 2011)

Saving Wildlife: Rainforest Animals by Sonya Newland (Watts, 2010)

Voices of the Rainforest by Mick Manning and Brita Granstrom (Watts, 2007)

Glossary

archaeologist a scientist who studies the remains of past civilisations.

bauxite a mineral used to make aluminium

basin the total area drained by a river and its tributaries.

buttress roots tree roots that stick out like a rocket fins, to support the weight of a large tree.

canopy the dense layer of leaves high above the ground in a forest.

channel the passage through which a river flows.

cholera a disease of the gut.

climate the long-term weather pattern in a region.

convert to change something into something else, or to change someone's religious beliefs.

current a regular flow of water in a certain direction.

dam a barrier that diverts or holds back water.

delta a flat, swampy area of land that forms as a river drops silt at its mouth.

descend to go down.

downstream towards the mouth of the river

dredge to deepen or widen a river by digging, to make it easier for ships to pass.

ecotourism a type of tourism that aims to protect the environment.

environment the surroundings in which plants, animals and people live.

floodplain the flattish land on either side of a river which often floods after heavy rain.

generate to make.

gorge a deep, narrow valley with sheer sides.

habitat a particular place where certain plants and animals live, such as a rainforest or desert.

illegal something that is against the law.

infertile of soil that is too poor to produce healthy crops.

hydroelectricity electricity that is made using energy from fast-flowing water.

latex the white, milky sap from rubber trees, which is used to make rubber.

malaria a disease carried by mosquitoes.

meander a looping bend on a river.

nutrients nourishment.

preserve to save.

rapids an area of white water where a river crashes over rocks.

reserve a protected area.

reservoir an artificial lake used to store water, made by damming a river or stream.

resources useful materials, such as timber and minerals.

sap watery liquid in plants that carrys nutrients such as sugars, salts and minerals

silt fine sand or mud carried along by a river.

terrain the lie of the land.

tributary a minor river or stream that joins the main river.

tuber the fleshy stem or root of a plant.

turbine a machine powered by steam, gas or water that is used to generate electricity.

upstream towards the source of the river

Index